The Westward Journey

Kristian Hvidt

The Westward Journey

The Dream of America

℃ Creative Education

The Dream of America

The series consists of

 1 Europe and the Flight to America
 2 America Fever
 3 The Westward Journey
 4 They Came to America
 5 Gateway to America: New York City
 6 Shattered Dreams: Joe Hill
 7 Ireland in Flight

Editor (Danish edition): Flemming Lundahl
Picture Editor: Anita Amundsen
Covers: Nancy Arend
English Edition translated and edited by J. R. Christianson & Birgitte Christianson
Cover photo: USIS

Danish Edition © 1976 by Munksgaard/Copenhagen
English Edition © 1982 by Creative Education, Inc.

Library of Congress Catalog Card No.: 81-71512
Author: Hvidt, Kristian
       The westward journey.
Mankato, MN: Creative Education, Inc.
96 P.
8201   811124
ISBN: 0-87191-707-6

Contents

emigrant = a person who leaves
   a country
immigrant = a person who comes
   into a country
migrant = a person who moves
   around within a country

The same person could be all three,
leaving their native land first, then
coming to America, and then mov-
ing from state to state inside
America.

The Mighty Ocean

Fear of Sailing the Atlantic

The gold of California and the fertile soil of the Midwest tempted millions of poor Europeans in the 1800's. You can read how news was spread about the wonders of America in the book, *America Fever*, in this series on *The Dream of America*.

But many doubts had to be overcome before these poor Europeans would arrive at the decision to leave their homelands. Part of the fear was the thought of the voyage across the great Atlantic Ocean. The thought of a little ship on those big waves, of drowning and of seasickness, could make many a bright dream fade away.

There were good reasons to be afraid of the voyage across the Atlantic a century ago. But most of the emigrants were afraid out of ignorance, not out of knowledge of the sea. They came from farming areas in the middle of the continent. Their first sight of open

A stormy day on the "Hekla," in the spring of 1862

water was often the trip across the North Sea. This could be unpleasant enough, but it was nothing compared to what the emigrants discovered when they met the great, roaring Atlantic Ocean.

It is hard for us to imagine how violent this ocean seemed in the past. There is a distance of about 6,000 km from the western coasts of Europe to the eastern shores of America. This distance is usually covered in about seven hours by one of the many daily airline flights from Europe to New York. Seen from an altitude of 10,000 meters, the ocean looks quite peaceful. But down on the water itself, in a small sailing vessel of the 1800's, the experience is something else—and much less peaceful.

One sign of how strong the forces were that drove the migration to America is the fact that these millions of people actually dared to sail across the Atlantic.

Storm and Fog, Icebergs and Shoals

Storms are often considered to be the greatest threat to a ship, but in the past, fog was considered just as dangerous. Many wrecks took place in fog when ships ran into the rocky shoals that jut out of the ocean. In the Atlantic, the areas west of Ireland are especially dangerous. But icebergs were every bit as dangerous as foggy weather. Thousands of icebergs are formed in the area between Greenland and Canada. They flow south with the cold water of the Labrador Current. When this current meets the warm water of the Gulf Stream, dense fog forms and the icebergs collect in the foggy area. This occurs on the direct route between Europe and America.

In the spring when the immigrant traffic was at its height, the fog was often dense off the coast of Newfoundland. This forced the ships to take a longer route some 100 km to the south. However, when a new ship was trying to break the record for speed in crossing the Atlantic, the captain sometimes defied the dangers of icebergs. He sailed straight through the waters off Newfoundland. The result was a series of horrible shipwrecks with thousands of casualties. Icebergs

The coastal waters off Newfoundland are dangerous. Fog often hides the icebergs and the rocky coast. This shows one of the first steamships, wrecked off the coast of Newfoundland in the summer of 1849.

and shoals caused wrecks more often than storms.

Storms could throw a ship off course. Storms could torture ships and their passengers. The crossing could be lengthened by weeks and even months. However, when emigration really took hold in the 1860's, most ships were so big that even the waves of an Atlantic storm could no longer tip them over very easily.

8

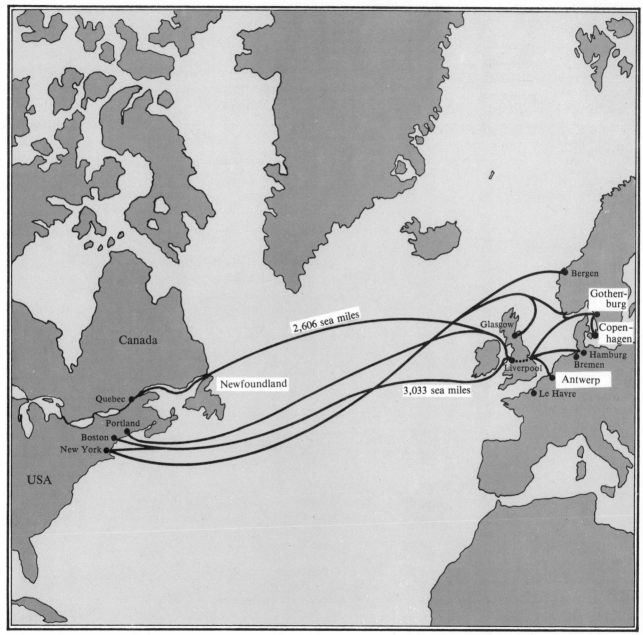

The routes from Europe to America

From Sail to Steam

Fifty-two million people, representing a large percentage of the total population of Europe, were transported across the Atlantic within about 75 years. During these same years, there were dramatic developments in sea transportation.

American Sailing Ships

Until the middle of the 1800's, almost all transportation over the Atlantic was by sailing ship. Sailing ships had been much improved in the course of time. Americans were especially skilled ship builders. Their ships were long, narrow and streamlined. They had more masts and sails than other ships.

Mass transportation of people across the Atlantic was not a new activity in the early 1800's. The slave trade between Africa and the New World provided lots of experience in mass "passenger" traffic. Slaves were considered to be a perishable cargo. Slave ships had to be able to sail quickly from one continent to another before the slaves died. The ships had to be streamlined for speed, but not too narrow or the hold would become too small and they would roll too much in the sea, making their human cargo sick.

American Clipper ship, the "Electra," 1850. These streamlined vessels with many sails were the fastest ships on the ocean before steamships.

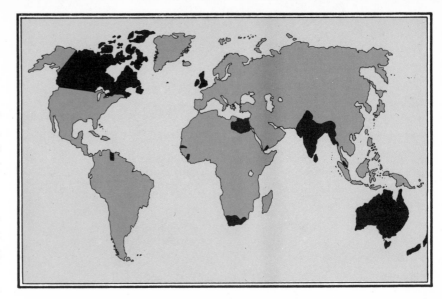

Americans competed with Englishmen in the importing of tea from China. For this purpose, the Americans built elegant four masted ships, the China Clippers. They were exceptionally fast. Some ships of a similar type also sailed the Atlantic when the first wave of emigrants were being transported in the 1830's.

These fast ships could sail from England to America in about three weeks with favorable winds. They were not very comfortable ships for passengers, however. Space was very limited, the ship rolled with the waves and took in much water. Everything on board was constantly wet in bad weather.

Many still preferred to travel with these ships instead of the broader and more stable ones that took a month or more to reach New York. Sometimes when conditions were unfavorable, the voyage might take up to sixty days.

During the era of sailing ships, Americans dominated the business of transporting emigrants. As late as 1849, American ships carried 137,000 of the 200,000 emigrants from Europe in that year.

At that time, it was already apparent that sailing ships were doomed. In the long run, they would not be able to compete with the technological wonder of the day: the steamship.

Despite the fact that Americans were also innovators in the development of steamships, they lost the lead in trans-Atlantic steamship traffic. England came to dominate this field completely. And England's superiority in steamship transportation became vital to the unity of the great British Empire which spanned the whole world of the late 1800's.

Steamers became common on American rivers long before they were used on the ocean. As early as 1819, thirty-one steamboats sailed the Mississippi and other American rivers.

11

Steamboats on the Mississippi, 1859.

France, in thirty days. But that was just as long as a sailing ship took. What is more, the "Savannah" had only travelled under steam for 23 of the 30 days. Sails had to be used the rest of the time.

Another twenty years passed before technological improvements allowed a ship to sail under steam across the Atlantic. When that became possible, the travel time was reduced to about fifteen days.

Technological Problems

Even before 1800, there had been attempts to build ships powered by a steam engine. The first successful attempts were made on American rivers. The first practical steamship was Robert Fulton's "Claremont." From 1807 on, it sailed a regular route up and down the Hudson River from New York to Albany.

In the following years, the design of the paddlewheel steamer was perfected. Hundreds of them were built to provide transportation on the rivers of America, long before steamships came into use in Europe. Here in America, there

was easy access to coal and water, and the paddlewheel steamer used tremendous amounts of both. Steamships could not yet be used on the ocean because they could not carry enough coal, and salt water could not be used in the steam engine. Trans-Atlantic steam traffic only became possible when the steam condenser was invented. This allowed the water in the steam engine to circulate and be used again and again to form steam, driving the pistons of the engine.

A paddlewheel steamer called the "Savannah" was built in 1828. She was built to cross the Atlantic, and she did, reaching LaHavre,

12

Regular Steamship Traffic

The black smoke that billowed out of steamships, the rattle of the great paddlewheels, and the tight quarters in ships that had to carry so much coal—all of these disadvantages meant that sailing ships could still compete with steamers in the 1860's. The technological problems standing in the way of steam travel across the Atlantic were only slowly overcome. It took a long time before the military importance of steamships was recognized. The admirals of the great British navy did not want to see their beautiful old warships with their many sails and broadsides of cannons replaced by smoking tin cans.

A crucial difference between travel by sailing ship and travel by steamship was that the steamship could sail whenever it wished. Sailing ships had to wait until the wind was right. In transporting emigrants across the Atlantic, it was steamships that allowed regular sailing schedules to be established. The steamships departed, for example, three times a week at a time that could be scheduled exactly. This was impossible with sailing ships.

New York harbor in 1850. Steamships sailed up and down the Hudson River. Sailing ships crossed the Atlantic. In the background, the island of Manhattan.

13

Emigrant Life 1820-1850

Freight One Way,
Passengers the Other

As long as only a few thousand people emigrated each year, the large fleet of freighters furnished transportation for them. These ships brought cotton and tobacco from the southern states to Europe, or lumber from Canada. When the ships sailed back, passengers were simply loaded into the hold. While these American sailing ships were unloading in the harbors of Europe, the captain went around to the inns and hotels of the area and recruited passengers for the return voyage. In Norway, they traveled far into the mountain valleys looking for emigrants to fill their ships. This recruitment by ship captains touched off the ''America fever'' that soon infected all of Europe. As for the captains themselves, the reason they were willing to spend so much time looking for passengers was undoubtedly because they could put the ticket money in their own pocket.

Ship owners, however, quickly discovered that transporting emigrants could be a good business. A ship full of passengers gave more profit than any other kind of cargo. All they had to do was pack them tightly into the hold.

Norwegian emigrants leave home, 1843.

English emigrants on their way to the port city in 1850.

Emigrant Ships

Gradually, real passenger ships began to be built, ships that were permanently fitted out for passengers. They were arranged in two classes:

First class, with ten or twenty cabins on the deck for the more wealthy passengers.

Second or Emigrant class, called steerage in advertisements. This was the hold itself, filled with passengers on one or two deck levels.

The whole world was talking about the giant ship, "Great Eastern," in 1861. It was built in England to sail to New York. This great steamship was almost 200 meters long. The first class passengers had spacious sitting rooms like the one in this picture.

Freighters in those days could quickly be converted into passenger ships. All it took was some lumber and canvas. First the hold was divided into two sections, one for men and one for women. Then several rows of wide shelves were erected along the walls. These served as bunks. It could all be quickly put up and just as quickly taken down again when the ship was to be loaded with cotton, tobacco or lumber for the return trip to Europe.

Slaves ships had been fitted out in the same way.

15

Emigrants in steerage in the 1860's.

Some ships could carry 1,000 passengers. In order to do that, however, the steerage decks had to be crowded with passengers in a manner that resembled the slave ships of a century earlier.

Ports of Departure

The largest port of departure for emigrant ships leaving Europe was originally Rotterdam in the Netherlands. Many emigrants came there from Germany and France. They sailed down the Rhine River, which meets the sea at Rotterdam. But the Dutch did very little to help the emigrants, who were usually poor people. When the flight to America began on a really large scale in the 1830's, the Netherlands lost this important source of income.

LeHavre in France was also an important port of emigration in the early days. Many of the first emigrants from northern Europe sailed to America by way of LeHavre. Later, they sailed by way of Hamburg or Bremen instead. These two cities had been Germany's biggest ports for many years. As early as the beginning of the 1850's, 80,000 Germans and Scandinavians sailed from Hamburg and Bremen each year.

However, neither Bremen nor Hamburg had enough ships for the rising tide of emigrants. Therefore, many German emigrants crossed over to England and departed for America from the port of Liverpool. The first groups of Danish Mormons traveled this route. First they took a ship from Copenhagen

The harbor at Hamburg. Emigrants are being ferried out to their ship.

17

to Kiel in Germany. From there, they took the train to Hamburg, and from there, they sailed to Hull in England. Then they took the train across England to Liverpool. From Liverpool, the ship sailed directly to America.

England was and remained Europe's greatest sea power. Liverpool became the dominant port for travel to America. There were historic reasons for this. Liverpool had been the contact port between the textile mills of the English Midlands and the cotton fields of the American South for over a century. Slave transportation was also part of Liverpool's shipping business. As late as 1807, the year in which England abolished the slave trade, 185 ships of Liverpool had managed to transport a total of 49,213 slaves from Africa to the Americas. It was natural that this same city, thirty or forty years later, had the ships and experience to dominate the mass transportation of emigrants across the Atlantic.

Departure from Liverpool.

The cabin of a ship sailing between Copenhagen and Kiel, 1829.

On Board an Emigrant Ship in 1847

In the year 1847, Liverpool suddenly had real need for its experience from the days of the slave trade. In that year, tens of thousands of poor people streamed into Liverpool from Ireland. The potato harvest had failed. The eight million people of Ireland were suffering a tremendous famine. All who could afford to fled the country. Many of them headed for America by way of Liverpool.

Irish local authorities and landlords solved the problem of famine by giving out free tickets to America. This seemed to be the best way to help the poor. No food was available, even if you had the money to buy it. So thousands of poor Irish gathered in Liverpool harbor. Shipping companies had to use all available ships to get the Irish off to America. The problems in Ireland in these years are discussed in the book *Ireland in Flight*, in this series on *The Dream of America*.

Emigrants wave good-bye. The crowd on board shows how many people the ships carried. This ship is leaving Liverpool in December, 1844.

The cost of a ticket was very low, but conditions on board were also very bad. The hold was divided into "bunks" 180 by 180 cm in size—about the size of a small double bed. Four adults or three adults and two children were assigned to each bunk. The bunks were built in two or three layers, each about 90 cm above the other. With a very narrow passage down the center of the ship between these rows of bunks, the steerage area could be made to contain up to 1,000 emigrants. There were no windows or portholes in steerage. Ladders led up to a few hatches in the deck above. Light came from a few oil or petroleum lamps hanging from nails in the ceiling. In the bunk, each of the four passengers had less than one square meter of space. Mattress and bedding were not included. The emigrants had to bring their own.

It does not take much imagination to see how awful these quarters must have been, even under the best of conditions. In a storm on the open Atlantic, they became almost unbearable. All the hatches had to be closed during a storm, because the waves rolled in over the deck. The passengers rolled back and forth in their narrow bunks. The lack of fresh air

Steerage on an emigrant ship in 1844. The bunks along the sides hold four people in every compartment. This drawing makes it look much more cozy and friendly than it really was.

increased seasickness and made the air extremely foul and nauseating. There were usually about four or five toilets in outhouses up on deck. They were used by hundreds of people, but they could not be used when the weather was even slightly stormy. Then the hatches were locked and the steerage passengers had to remain in their quarters. No wonder these emigrant ships often had epidemics of infectious diseases. If cholera or typhus started on a ship, it could

really thin out the number of passengers in steerage during the course of a month's voyage.

Meals on board were important times of the day. Every morning, the emigrants stood in line on deck. The food was passed out. There was fresh water, oatmeal, slab meat or fish, hardtack and perhaps some molasses. There was a galley on deck—a kitchen with a range. Each family could take their turn and prepare their meal. But there were many people to share

the same pots and pans, and it was difficult to cook when the ship was rocking up and down in the big waves of the open ocean.

Good health was necessary to survive these weeks at sea, and more than ordinary good humor was needed to live for a month under these crowded conditions, together with 1,000 other people. You had to put up with it: there was no way to get off the ship in mid-ocean.

Daily life in steerage during the voyage to America.

An English writer who had experienced this nightmare wrote, "Before the emigrant has been one week on the ocean, he is another person. How could it be otherwise? Hundreds of poor people, men, women and children of all ages from newborn infant to elderly, are packed together like sardines in a can. They live without light, without air, covered with filth and forced to breathe the foul fumes of the chamber pots. They are broken down by seasickness. These people are marked for the rest of their lives by the experience."

At least five million English, Irish, Germans and Scandinavians willingly embarked on this voyage over the Atlantic in sailing ships before 1860. The ocean claimed

Open fires in stoves on wooden ships often caused fires. This picture shows the burning frigate, "Ocean Monarch," about to disappear into the ocean.

A storm tore the rigging off the American ship, "Henry Clay," in 1845.

22

about 5%-10% of these people. In the years 1847-1853, fifty-nine emigrant ships disappeared beneath the waves. Besides those who went down with their ship, there were hundreds who died of typhus or cholera on board ships that made it to America.

The mere fact that so many emigrants dared to embark on such a voyage shows how desperately they needed to get away from the privations and sufferings at home.

Furthermore, they did not really know how far it actually was to America. There are many stories of emigrants who started looking for the skyline of New York three or four days after their ship had left harbor.

The complaints of emigrants who made it to America often in- cluded stories of how roughly cap- tains and crews of emigrant ships treated the passengers. The sailors certainly were a rough bunch in those days. They had to live most of their lives in the dangerous con- ditions that were a part of daily life at sea. No wonder the sailors who opened the continent of America to Europeans were a raw and rug- ged lot.

Even in stormy weather, sailors had to work with the sails up on the masts and yardarms.

Everyday life on an emigrant ship, showing the various types of emigrants from the 1860's.

The First Emigrants From Norway and Denmark

The ocean was something new for most people from farms and cities. Farmers knew no more about the ocean than their hogs or chickens did. The emigrants had strong and hard muscles, used to the work of breaking rocks and felling trees, but these muscles were of no use on the ocean. Everyone was equally helpless at sea. Even the best of farmers was not worth much on a swaying bunk.

Emigration from Norway in 1825

The ocean was not completely unknown to all farmers, however. In Norway, arms of the sea reach far into the land in the deep fjords. Farmers along the fjords were in closer contact with the outside world. This is probably part of the reason why Norway began to send out a stream of emigrants so early. The beginning of organized emigration from Norway was in 1825. Fifty-two Norwegians purchased the sloop, "Restauration," and sailed to New York after a voyage of more than three months. In the years following, hundreds of others left Norway—some traveled from Liverpool in English ships.

The Emigrants From Denmark Who Ended in Spain

Denmark also attempted an early group emigration in the style of the Norwegians. The idea came from a furniture manufacturer named Dessau, who lived in the town of Aarhus in the late 1830's. He gathered about fifty people who wanted to go to the New World. He sold his house and bought a schooner, "Die Elbe," for the money. This ship was to take the group to America.

It turned out to be a sad story. The emigrants from Aarhus made it out of the English Channel, but the ship sailed poorly on the open Atlantic. Winds drove them down into the Bay of Biscay. When the ship approached the northern coast of Spain, it was plundered by Spanish soldiers. The voyage went no farther. Some of the people stayed in Spain. Others returned home to Denmark in desperate straits.

25

Emigration Laws

The story of Dessau's emigration fiasco reached Denmark and created much discussion. A contemporary play mentioned it. The case was also investigated by the authorities. There was a debate over whether or not the government should step in to protect citizens from sailing to America in ships that were too small or otherwise unsuitable. The final decision was that the government should not get involved.

"Liberalism" was becoming strong as a political philosophy in the 1830's. This philosophy dominated until 1900. The main idea was that the government should leave people alone and not get involved in the protection of its citizens by means of legislation.

At the same time, one report after another began to arrive from America. There were reports of emigrants from Europe who had arrived in America more dead than alive because of starvation, seasickness, illness and filth. All of this was because ship owners crowded more and more people into their ships in order to earn more money.

Mandatory medical examinations for emigrants were introduced at Liverpool in 1844. But they were not very thorough. A single doctor might have to check more than 1,000 emigrants in a day.

After many of these reports came back, ordinary human compassion for fellow countrymen won out over the principles of liberalism. One country after another began to pass laws to protect emigrants.

It began in England, where the hordes of Irish emigrants in particular were badly treated. The British Passengers Act stated that every ship had to bring a certain amount of fresh water, hardtack, salt meat, etc., per passenger. The amount of space per passenger in steerage was also regulated. Men and women could no longer be put in the same bunk unless they were married.

The British Law did not help the emigrants a great deal because there was no provision for its enforcement. But it was an important law anyway, because it served as a model for legislation in other European countries. Protection of emigrants was necessary because they were completely helpless in the hands of those who sold tickets to America. A ship owner or captain could tell them whatever they wanted to, but when the ship left harbor, the emigrant was helpless in the hands of the captain.

Other European countries copied the British law during the following years. Emigration laws

An advertisement's peek through the portholes of an English emigrant ship. On the left, the cabin for unmarried women; middle, the family cabin; right, the bachelors' quarters.

were passed in Hamburg and Bremen in 1853, Norway in 1857, and Sweden in 1866. All ships had to be inspected before departure. That helped somewhat. But no law could hinder a ship owner from promising a paradise on board ship or gold and green acres when they arrived in America. Every ship owner was anxious to sell more and more tickets to America, and they kept on using extravagant promises to do so.

When young Peter in Christian Winther's poem, "The Flight to America," wanted to persuade his little brother to go to America with him, he used the language of a ticket seller:

"But when you make it over there
They give you a plantation free
And you will never have to care
For money grows on bush and tree.

The horses all wear silver shoes
And wagon wheels are silver too.
Gold nuggets lie around to choose,
You just bend down and take a few."

In the 1800's, you could honestly say, "People are free to emigrate to America." But what if they were lured away with false promises by those who profited from taking them there? Did the liberal ideals of a free market apply here too? This was a real problem to people in the 1800's. The result of this problem was that European emigration laws turned out to be halfhearted attempts to protect innocent emigrants from fraud. In reality, the laws were so weak that they were of little value.

The Danish Emigration Law of 1868

A typical example of emigration legislation is the law passed in Denmark in 1868. This law came after a long series of complaints to the authorities about the way Danish emigrants were treated on the voyage to America. The Danish consul general in New York saw examples of Danes who arrived in America on English or German ships, starved and broken down physically. There were more Danes on poor relief in New York than there were Norwegians and Swedes put together.

The Ottawa Affair— A Scandal

An affair in 1866 paved the way for the Danish Emigration Law. This was the so-called Ottawa Affair. A company suddenly appeared in 1864 that called itself "The American Company for the Acquisition of Property." It was supported by a number of prominent Danish businessmen. The aim of the company was to get people to emigrate to America. The company advertised that it owned large tracts of fertile land in Texas, where a Norwegian colony had already been established. This advertising was so successful that

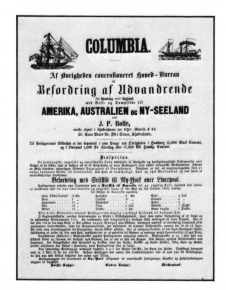

An advertisement for emigrants. Around 1870, thousands of handbills like this were circulated.

the company chartered a whole ocean liner, the "Ottawa." It sailed to America with 100 Danes and 400 Swedish and Norwegian emigrants.

The ship made it to New York, but by then the glitter was gone from the project. Nobody in New York knew anything about the land in Texas. In the meantime, the company in Denmark had gone bankrupt. The leaders of the group had no money to transport the emigrants farther than New York.

Most of these 500 immigrants had come to America on credit. The company had sold tickets on the installment plan: so much down and the rest later. Furthermore, the "Ottawa" had not been paid for, and the crew was demanding their wages.

Money was needed immediately. So the leaders of the group raised it in an unusual way. They "sold" all of the immigrants to an agent. He was hiring workers for a railroad. All but about 100 of the "Ottawa" passengers ended in Missouri.

The emigrant ship, "Ottawa," leaves Copenhagen on its first—and last—trip to America in 1866.
The whole scheme turned out to be a fraud.

Florida was a swampy wilderness in the 1800's. Because of malaria, no white people went there by choice, but a number of the Ottawa passengers ended their days in Florida.

There they were grossly underpaid for laying rails—but the company in Missouri paid the Danish-American company $5,000 for the immigrants.

The situation was even worse for the remaining 100 passengers from the "Ottawa." They were sent to Florida, which was almost uninhabited at that time. Malaria and other tropical diseases were rampant. The first white settlers in Florida used Native Americans and immigrants to drain the immense swamps. In order to eliminate malaria, the malaria mosquito had to be wiped out. These mosquitoes bred in the swamps. How many of the 100 immigrants survived this work in the Florida swamps is unknown. They simply disappeared from history.

Police Regulation

The Ottawa Affair led to the Danish Emigration Law. This law was to prevent such irresponsible treatment of the country's respected, but perhaps naive, citizens. The police made certain that agents did not promise more than they could deliver. The law of May 1, 1868, stated that all emigrants had to have their travel contract (that is, their ticket) checked by the Copenhagen police. The travel route, the day of departure, and the expenses on route that were included in the ticket were all guaranteed by police before the voyage began. If the contract was not fulfilled, for example if the emigrant did not get on the ship promised or if they did not get the food they had been promised, they could complain to the Danish consul when they arrived in America. The police in Denmark would then bring charges against the agent. The police retained a copy of all emigration contracts.

In order to control the agents of shipping companies, the law also stated that all agents had to be approved by the police. An agent had to be licensed, and he had to post a large bond with the police. This bond was to guarantee repayment to emigrants whose contracts were not fulfilled. The authorities would not risk another situation like the Ottawa Affair. Passengers must not be left holding the bag if an agent went bankrupt.

A page from the emigration protocol of the Copenhagen police, 1883. Computer analysis of these records has been used to determine who the Danish emigrants were and where they came from.

The law also stated that the police had to inspect the ships that carried emigrants. However, these rules only covered ships that sailed directly from Denmark to America. It gave security to only a small percentage of Danish emigrants. Most Danish emigrants boarded the ships that took them to America in foreign ports like Hamburg or Liverpool. Their contracts were only protected by whatever laws existed in those countries.

The Police Archives

The Danish Emigration Law of 1868 was certainly meant well, but whether or not it had any real influence on the welfare of emigrants is debatable. However, we can be thankful that the law was passed, though for a completely different reason: it has provided excellent records for modern historians. The provision that all contracts had to go through the police office means that excellent records of emigration were kept for the whole period after 1868. Copies of the contracts were not kept. They were too bulky and were disposed of by the police after a certain period of time. But the police kept a record of the name and departure date of every single emigrant, as well as other essential information. These records still exist.

Many Danish Americans have found their Danish roots by using these records. However, the information in these protocols has to be used carefully. It is possible to find out how old the emigrants were when they left Denmark. But the protocols list an unusual number of infants under one year of age, and an equally large number of ten to eleven year old boys and girls. There were almost no children twelve to thirteen years old. What could be the reason for this? The answer is simple. A child's ticket cost half the price of an adult ticket. At the age of twelve, you had to pay the full price. There are few twelve and thirteen year olds listed because parents said they were a year or two younger so that they could travel for half price. Babies under one year of age travelled free, then as now, when accompanied by their mothers.

Mass Emigration at Full Steam

The mail steamer, "Britannia," built in 1840. She was one of the first steamships on the trans-Atlantic route.

In the 1850's, almost all emigrants sailed across the Atlantic in large three and four masted sailing ships. Around 1850, competition in speed developed between the American and English sailing ships. The Gold Rush to California encouraged thousands of adventurers from all of Europe to head for the New World.

Crossing the North American continent was very hard at that time. It was faster to sail all the way around South America and up the Pacific coast to California. A special type of clipper ship was developed for this voyage. The voyage around South America took two months from New York. In addition, future gold diggers had to spend at least one month on board a ship from Europe to America. The desire to strike it rich in the gold fields must have been very strong.

Mail Carriers Over The Atlantic

Soon the steamships began to appear as competition. The first successful steamship company for transportation across the Atlantic was established by Samuel Cunard in 1839. This company, the Cunard Line, is still among the greatest shipping companies of the world. Cunard won the right to carry mail across the Atlantic.

The right to carry mail gave a tremendous profit to the company. So other companies competed for the right. The mail contract was given to the company that could sail most quickly from England to the USA. This was the background to the great trans-Atlantic races between passenger liners sailing the route from Europe to America. The Atlantic Blue Ribbon was the symbol of the speed record. This

33

competition was front page news in the world press until after the Second World War. Then the passenger liner finally gave way to the airplane.

The race began in 1850, when some Americans established a competing line, the Collin Line, to challenge Cunard. This American line built the fastest ships, so they took over the right to carry mail.

America Drops Out of the Atlantic Traffic

During the early years, the passenger routes lost money. The ships used too much coal and the room for passengers was too small. The cost of a ticket was too high for the poorer emigrants. The passenger routes were kept going by the income from carrying mail. The American Collin Line and the English Cunard Line were in fierce competition for a number of years. In the end, Collin lost out. After two shipwrecks, the public was afraid to sail with Collin. Cunard won, but it soon had to face even harder competition.

When the Collin Line lost out to Cunard, America dropped out of the emigrant traffic. Political tensions in the USA led to the Civil

34

Cunard Line was the largest passenger line, and it also owned the largest ships.

The Cunard Line office in Copenhagen in 1918.

Foreign language newspapers in America carried many advertisements for Atlantic travel. Immigrants could send tickets to friends and relatives in the Old Country, and some could even afford a trip back to visit their native land.

War in 1861. American merchant ships were not ready to compete when the European mass emigration really set in, and after the Civil War, it was more profitable for Americans to build railroads in the west than to build ships for emigrants. English and German shipping lines transported most of the many millions of Europeans who sailed westwards. And they made money doing it. The final victory of the steamship over the sailing ship took place in the late 1860's.

Norwegian data shows how quickly it happened. In 1867, only 10% of the Norwegian emigrants travelled by steamship to America, while 90% travelled with sailing ships. Four years later, in 1871, only 33% came to America under sail, while 67% now came on steamships. Even though it was more expensive to travel by steamship to America, it was worth it.

A Norwegian newspaper put it this way in 1867: "The emigrant can arrive in America in good health when travelling by steamship. His will and energy have not been weakened by a long, dull and often unhealthy stay on board a sailing ship. It costs about fourteen dollars to take a sailing ship if you furnish your own food. The food is worth another eight dollars. The voyage usually takes a month, but you have to be prepared to spend two months at sea. A steamship ticket costs about thirty dollars, but then everything is included from the time you leave Christiania (now Oslo), and the trip only takes about fourteen days."

The sailing ships tried to compete by lowering prices. They could not afford to sail half empty across the Atlantic. But lower prices did not help. Within less than ten years, they were completely out of the passenger business on the trans-Atlantic route. In 1875, more than 95% of the emigrants were sailing by steamship.

English Passenger Lines

The triumph of the Cunard Line lasted only a short time. In the years to come, a number of strong

INMAN LINIEN.
KONGELIGE ENGELSKE POST DAMPSKIBE.

CITY OF ANTWERP
CITY OF BALTIMORE
CITY OF BROOKLYN
CITY OF BRUSSELS
CITY OF CORK
CITY OF DUBLIN
CITY OF DURHAM
ETNA

CITY OF HALIFAX
CITY OF LIMERICK
CITY OF LONDON
CITY OF MANCHESTER
CITY OF MONTREAL
CITY OF NEW YORK
CITY OF PARIS
CITY OF WASHINGTON

LIVERPOOL, NEW YORK & PHILADELPHIA DAMPSKIBSSELSKAB.

DISSE BEQVEMME OG VEL INDRETTEDE DAMPSKIBE EXPEDERES FRA

LIVERPOOL
TIL
NEW YORK
TO GANGE UGENTLIG.

GJENNEMGAAENDE BILLETTER SÆLGES TIL BILLIGST BEREGNEDE

Priser til CHICAGO, WINONA, RED WING, ST. PAUL, LANSING, MILWAUKEE, LA CROSSE,

OG TIL SAMTLIGE BYER I VESTSTATERNE.

EMIGRANTERNE BLIVE BEHANDLEDE MED OPMERKSOMHED.

DISSE DAMPSKIBE HENREGNES BLANDT DE STÖRSTE, HURTIGSTE OG BEQVEMMEST INDRETTEDE.

Man henvender sig i

WILLIAM INMAN'S EXPEDITION,
No. 7, QVÆSTHUSGADE, KJOBENHAVN,
GENERAL AGENTUR FOR DANMARK.

competitors appeared, both in England and in Germany. Some of them were new companies, but others were sailing companies that had gone over to steamships.

Many ships of other lines sailed from Liverpool as the Cunard ships did. One of the strongest competitors was the Inman Line. It took the Atlantic Blue Ribbon away from Cunard in the 1870's. In 1879, Inman advertised the first ship with electric lights. Other companies were the National Line and the Dominion Line, which both originally sailed to the southern ports of New Orleans and Galveston. Later, they sailed to northern ports and to Canada.

White Star Line was originally a company with sailing ships that ran to Australia. When it looked like there was more money to be earned by transporting emigrants to America, the White Star Line began sailing to New York and Philadelphia. White Star Line was owned by the famous T. H. Ismay after 1867. The greatest ships after 1900 carried the White Star symbol on their smokestacks. The "Titanic" was a White Star ship. The

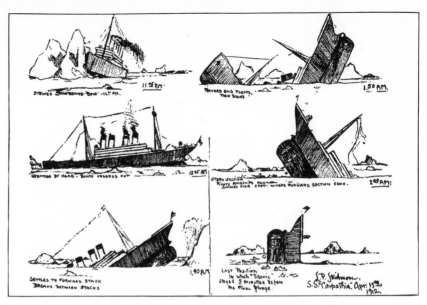

One of the worst sea catastrophes of all times was in 1912, when the "Titanic" hit an iceberg and went down in a matter of two hours. In an attempt to break the trans-Atlantic speed record, she had sailed straight through the thick fog off Newfoundland.

whole world was shocked in 1912 when this great steamship crashed into an iceberg off the coast of Newfoundland and sank with 1200 passengers. This was one of the worst sea catastrophes in history.

The Canadian Route

Two major shipping companies sailed out of Glasgow in Scotland. These were the Anchor Line and the Allan Line. The Allan Line had been founded in 1819 and had earned large profits by sailing to Irish ports. It had carried a large

percentage of the emigrants who left Ireland. The Allan Line also became important in Scandinavia. It became one of the largest passenger lines in the world in the years when Norwegians, Danes and Swedes were emigrating by the tens of thousands every year. The special feature of these two Glasgow companies was that they landed their passengers in Canada, either Halifax, Nova Scotia, or in the city of Quebec on the St. Lawrence River. The distance from Glasgow to Canada was much shorter than to New York. Consequently, the Scottish routes

The Inman Line was the next oldest English passenger line. This line had the first ship with propellers instead of paddlewheels.

Sailing on the Mississippi, with its shifting sandbars, was just as hard as sailing the Atlantic. Here, the paddlewheel steamer, "Iowa," moves through an obstacle in 1876.

were cheaper. The passengers did not settle in Canada. Most of them went on, by train or Great Lakes steamer, to the United States. The route from Glasgow to Quebec and on to Chicago was actually the most direct connection to the prairie states of the Midwest.

German Passenger Lines

The German passenger lines also played an important role in the transportation of emigrants. The Hamburg-America Line in Hamburg and the North German Lloyd in Bremen became large and influential companies in the economic life of northern Europe. The Bremen line carried 60,000 to 70,000 emigrants to America every year during the 1880's.

These two companies competed with each other. They alternated in superiority. Their ships were the pride of all Germany. Germany was attempting to become a world power during those years. The passenger lines got big loans from the government to build grand new ships. These ships were named for members of the German imperial family, and every time one was launched, it was the occasion for a national festival in Germany. They were beautiful ships from the outside. The rich passengers in first class had luxurious accommodations. But in steerage, among the emigrants, there were very cramped quarters. The German companies earned their money by offering cheap mass transportation to the steerage passengers.

The North Sea Route to Hull

Most of the thousands of Scandinavian emigrants chose to depart from Liverpool. Their journey began in a Scandinavian port like Gothenburg, Bergen or Copenhagen, and went from there to England, usually to Hull. This leg of the journey was usually on an English ship. Wilson Line was the main carrier on these North Sea routes. It had been founded in the 1820's. A son of the founder settled in Gothenburg, Sweden. He exported oats and beef to England in his father's ships. Later, the Wilson Line made a deal with the big trans-Atlantic lines in Liverpool that gave them the right to carry passengers from Scandinavia to Hull. The Wilson Line ships were converted from freighters into passenger ships. There were

38

many complaints about the way this line treated its passengers, and especially about conditions in Hull. The emigrants had to stay overnight there before taking the train to Liverpool the next day. But there was a serious shortage of hotel rooms in Hull. In the spring of 1881, for example, almost 53,000 Scandinavians passed through the city. Many of them had to spend the night outdoors, sleeping on their boxes and baggage.

Farewell sermon for emigrants departing from Gothenburg in May, 1869.

Larger and Faster Ships

Transportation across the North Atlantic changed the course of world history in the nineteenth and twentieth centuries. This great migration from Europe to America would never have been possible without the rapid technological revolution that altered the nature of ocean navigation.

Industrial Growth

This revolution did not simply make it easier to transport large numbers of people. It was also of fundamental importance to the development of industry. The great industrial areas of Germany and England were based on mass production. This assumed that the goods could be sold far from the area where they were produced. In order for mass production to be profitable, goods had to be sold over a wide area including foreign countries. Industry demanded the building of railroads and steamships to transport the goods.

The Technological Revolution

Ship owners grew rich. They used their money to improve and enlarge their fleets. Experiments were made with new motors and new types of ships. Steamships were improved from year to year. The passenger lines sailing between America and Europe were the leaders in these developments. It was on this route that the most money was earned. A shipment of emigrants made much more money

A Danish trans-Atlantic line was started in 1879. It was called the Thingvalla Line after its first ship. This painting shows its second ship, "Geiser," in 1882.

Propeller steamer and paddlewheel steamer competing with each other. The propeller ship won easily. But it was not until the 1860's that they found the right type of engine to drive the screw propeller. Experiments had begun as early as 1804.

for the company than a shipment of grain or industrial products.

The paddlewheel gave way to the screw propeller. Later, double propellers were invented. They increased the speed of a ship and decreased the consumption of coal. At the same time, improvements were made in steam engines. First came the high pressure steam engine, and then the steam turbine. All of this meant that the voyage from Europe could be made in less and less time.

The "Savannah" took twenty-nine days for the crossing in 1819. Twenty years later, in 1839, the crossing took fifteen days. By 1869, the record across the Atlantic from Liverpool to New York was eight days. New developments in the following years allowed

some ships of the 1890's to make the crossing in four and a half days. The distance over the Atlantic was still the same in miles, but in terms of travelling time, America and Europe moved much closer to each other within those few years.

The Atlantic steamships became larger and larger. In the early 1800's, sailors still thought the ships that Columbus had used to discover America were quite large. The "Savannah" was 350 tons

while the "Santa Maria" had been 250 tons. The length of ships was dependent on the size of trees. They could not increase above a certain size. But a steam hammer could produce iron sheets of almost any size. Iron ships could be built to an immense size. They were so huge that it was hard to launch them without tipping them over. Another practical problem was that the iron ships disturbed the compass.

	"Britannia," 1840	"Lusitania," 1906	"Queen Mary," 1934
Length	63 m	183 m	297 m
Breadth	10 m	20 m	36 m
Tonnage	1,154	12,950	80,744
Speed per hour	14 km	32 km	49 km

41

"Great Eastern," built 1861, was both a paddlewheel and propeller steamer. It could carry 4,000 passengers, but it turned out to be completely unsuited to the high waves of the North Atlantic.

The Economics of Passenger Transportation

The development of these great passenger ships was the result of three generations of technological progress. But the ships were also the result of money. Building these great luxury liners cost the passenger lines huge sums of money, and that money had to be earned back quickly. Money was needed to build newer, larger and faster ships. The bigger the ships got, and the more ships that were sailing the Atlantic, the more difficult it became to fill the ships with emigrants.

It was not easy to be the director of a big passenger line. The director had to assure that new ships were constantly being built. He had to place the orders for a new ship at just the right time. It could take three or four years to build a ship. In the meantime, economic conditions might change and there might be fewer emigrants to transport. Many rich and powerful passenger lines went bankrupt because of bad planning in their schedule for the launching of new ships.

Furthermore, wind and weather still caused problems. Despite bigger and stronger ships, there were still large and small catastrophes at sea. Often they hit shipping companies with a double blow. First, a ship was lost, and secondly, the accident might cause passengers to be afraid of the line and take other ships instead.

The greatest worry for the ship owner was always to get enough passengers. Other lines could "steal" emigrants by launching great advertising campaigns, or economic problems could hit either Europe or America. Then the number of emigrants decreased. The companies had to do something to assure a regular supply of emigrants so that they could afford to build and run their great ships with profit. Therefore, organizations were developed all over Europe to sell steamship tickets to America. Emigration became part of the business world—and a good business at that.

One single day of stormy weather on the Atlantic completely ruined the grand salon of the "Great Eastern."

43

Emigration Agent—A New Profession

Snaring Peasants

Along with the great migration from rural to urban areas came a number of agents, more or less honest as the case might be. They stationed themselves at the railroad stations and passenger ship docks in the big cities. They offered help to the men and women from the country. These country people did not know their way around the big city. But they came to settle in the city and seek their fortunes.

The agents spoke of "snaring peasants." In those days, there was no TV, no radio, and only a few newspapers, so people from the country had little opportunity to get information about life in a big city. Therefore they listened to the agents who offered to find them a job—or a ticket to the New World.

But the police were suspicious of the agents. In Denmark, the government asked the chief of police in Copenhagen in 1866 if there was any need for an emigration law. The answer was that there was a deep need for such a law.

"Because of the unbelievable recklessness with which the common people, in this and in much else, put themselves in the hands of almost any agent they chance to meet, and because of the unscrupulous ways by which dishonest and even notorious people take advantage of them in order to make money."

An emigration agent speaks to unemployed miners in Wales. In England, some of the labor unions had the rule that if unemployment reached a certain point, its members could get a free ticket to America or Australia.

New Emigration Agents

The first emigration agents offered all kinds of services to these people newly arrived in the city. They functioned as an employment agency, found people a place to live, and they could also sell tickets to America. They usually got their tickets through contacts in the great ports of emigration like Hamburg, Bremen and Liverpool.

Around 1867-1868, this situation changed drastically. A new type of emigration agent appeared. These new agents did not hang around railroad stations. They opened grand offices with big signs outside. These signs advertised the Cunard Line, the Inman Line, or the big Hamburg-America Line. And these were also the very years when emigration to America was increasing rapidly, when steamships were really starting to take over the traffic across the Atlantic. The major lines supported agents of their own because they wanted to assure themselves a large share of the flow of people.

In the big port cities of northern Europe, like Gothenburg, Oslo, Bergen, Copenhagen and Amsterdam, the major passenger lines appointed general agents. These were prominent individuals who were hired by the companies. They were often wealthy businessmen who

Copenhagen agency of the Hamburg-America Line around 1900.

Badge worn on the cap of one of Hornemann's "runners" in the 1860's, when he was by far the biggest general emigration agent in Copenhagen.

place where the future emigrants arrived in the city from the provinces. All local passenger ships docked in Nyhavn. Trains were not yet used in any great numbers because it was still easier and cheaper to sail.

Emigration was greatest in the spring. At that time of the year, thousands of people swarmed around Nyhavn. In the course of a single month, 10,000 to 15,000 Danes and Swedes could pass through the emigration agencies and small hotels of Nyhavn. This same kind of movement was repeated in great port cities all over Europe.

Emigrant runners had to be approved by the police after 1868. Then they all got a fancy badge for their caps.

Runners

All general agents employed people called "emigrant runners." They showed up every time a ship arrived from the provinces. Their job was to get as many emigrants as possible for their line. There must have been a good deal of yelling and shouting at these arrivals, when the future emigrants came down the gangplank with all their boxes, trunks, bundles and suitcases. They had packed for their whole future life. Therefore, they were easy to distinguish from the other passengers.

The battle now began between the runners to secure the most

had a large sum of money to invest. In Copenhagen, the first of these general agents for the Allan Line was Wilkens Hornemann. He opened his office in 1867, and soon other passenger lines followed with their own general agencies. Within a few years, the whole harbor area called Nyhavn was filled with emigration agencies representing all the big passenger lines.

This district became the center for emigration from all of Denmark and southern Sweden. The offices were located here in order to be as close as possible to the

passengers. Often, two runners pulled a new arrival in two different directions, trying to get him into the office of the Allan Line or the Hamburg-America Line. The police finally had to station guards by the ships. Many reports tell that the battle went on in the many small hotels where the emigrants stayed until they had found passage to America, or perhaps to Australia. Many hotel managers had arrangements with ticket agents to make sure that their guests bought tickets from a certain line.

The Trip to America— A Commodity

There was money to be earned from emigration. Every time a runner got somebody to purchase a ticket to America, the runner was paid a fee.

The trip to America was a commodity that could be bought and sold. This commodity was processed in several stages. First it went from the ship owner to his general agents all over Europe. From there, the commodity went out to a network of subagents or runners. There was a profit to be made at every stage. And all the money came from the emigrants who bought the tickets. The profit was very high, but a lot of hard work went into finding new customers for the trip to America. It makes you wonder whether the activities of these many agents all over Europe had a part in turning emigration into a mass movement.

General Agents

There were a number of general agents in every big European port city. They each represented one of the major passenger lines. The general agents were a very unusual group of people. Some were solid businessmen. But many of them had questionable backgrounds. Some were people with really bad reputations. Many of the general agents had spent some time in America. That was where they usually made contact with the passenger line that made them a general agent in their home country. Many of them were businessmen who had gone bankrupt, either at home or in America. They had to find a new job in another field, so they became general agents.

Posting Bond

A general agent needed money to get started. In Denmark, after the emigration law of 1868, a general agent had to put up as much as 10,000 dollars. That was a large sum of money. It did not have to be in cash, however. It could be in the form of a bond or a bank guarantee. This money was used as insurance to assure that the agent upheld the contracts he made with emigrants. If compensation had to be paid, the police could take it out of the sum on deposit. As far as we know, the police never actually did this. A few times, they did take steps leading to the dismissal of general agents who were too dishonest or had made other

The Hamburg-America Line was cheaper than the English lines, but it also gave poorer service. Here is their Copenhagen agency in the 1890's.

mistakes. But the evidence had to be overwhelming before the police would step in. One agent, for example, a representative of the Cunard Line, finally had his agency taken away from him when he was sent to prison for eight years.

The pawnshop was used by many poor people. Perhaps they could borrow enough money for the ticket to America by pawning their most valuable belongings.

A ship like the German vessel, "Northern Light," could be the subject of considerable debate. Was it safe or not? It sailed a direct route to New York in 1869-1872. It looks all right in this drawing, but is the drawing accurate?

A Typical Emigration Agent

Who was Vincent Riber?

It was a good job to be a general emigration agent.

Vincent Riber was born in 1835, the son of a doctor. He was trained as an electroplater. That was a brand new field at the time. It consisted of covering other metals with a thin layer of silver by means of electricity. This produced "silver plate" that looked just like solid sterling silver—until the plating wore off.

At the age of twenty, Riber emigrated to Australia in 1855. But he did not find happiness there, so he moved to New Zealand. He did not find the right opportunities there either, so he took the boat to America, where he stayed for eighteen years.

He made contact with the State Line passenger line in New York. This was one of the big Liverpool lines. In 1878, he came to Copenhagen as an employee of the State Line. The next year, Mr. Raffel, the sales director of the line, came to Copenhagen. He installed Riber as general agent for the State Line in Denmark.

Riber's contract with the State Line gives a good impression of how emigration looked through the eyes of a businessman. Riber had to be approved by the police and deposit a bond of 10,000 Danish crowns. He was not the one who actually put up the money.

All aboard! Emigrants haul their bags and boxes onto the steamer in Gothenburg, 1887.

The English company did that for him. In return, Riber had to pay 10,000 crowns of his own money to the company in Liverpool. This was a deposit for the money he would be taking in for tickets. The ticket receipts had to be sent to Liverpool once a month. According to this contract, Riber had full use of the State Line office in Copenhagen. The company paid all his office expenses. They also paid for all advertising, and that could be quite expensive. Riber received a salary of 100 English pounds a year, plus five shillings for each adult emigrant that he sent to America on State Line ships. An impression of how much this contract meant to Vincent Riber can be seen from what he earned in one year alone.

One Year's Income

The year 1883 was an ordinary emigration year. Riber sent 726 adults and 172 children to America that year. His main income would have been about 2,000 Danish crowns in base salary and about 8,120 crowns in fees for tickets sold. A general agent, however, had other sources of income as well. He exchanged money for emigrants and earned a small percentage on each dollar exchanged. Furthermore, many general agents functioned as a kind of banker as well. With the help of business connections in New York or Chicago, they sent out certificates of deposit, so that emigrants could pay a certain amount of money to the agent and have that same amount repaid to them in dollars when they arrived in America.

Finally, the general agent had one other source of income. He sold "emigration equipment" to be used on the voyage to America. As described on page 20, the emigrants had to prepare their own food on sailing ships. This was not true on steamships. The food was provided, but emigrants in steerage still had to furnish their own plate, cup, knife and fork. They also had to furnish their own bedding. Until the year 1900, there were not even mattresses on the bunks in steerage. All these things had to be purchased from the agent. It was almost like an addition to the ticket price. A mattress and pillow cost two crowns, a set of "tinware"—plate, cup and flatware—cost another two crowns. The agents also sold certain kinds of food like hardtack, crackers, etc., that the passengers could bring along to supplement the meals served on board.

All in all, Vincent Riber in a normal year would have had an income of about 12,000 Danish crowns. In the 1880's, that was a lot of money. To compare, a farm worker in the same year made about 250 or 300 crowns, a craftsman in Copenhagen about 750 crowns, and a supreme court justice earned 7,000 crowns a year. Riber's agency was not even a very large one. The Allan Line and White Star Line sent off three or four times as many emigrants each year.

Competition and Cooperation Between General Agents

Almost all general agents were in the same part of the city, and while they were out scouting for incoming emigrants, they also managed to keep an eye on each other. They kept track of whether other lines were secretly lowering prices to get more passengers. They kept track of the size of fees other general agents gave to their subagents and runners. Often, the general agents got into disputes with one another. They complained to the police and to their home offices in England or Germany. They asked for the same ticket prices and the same earnings as other general agents.

Sometimes the general agents tried to cooperate instead of competing with each other. They

Passagerer befordres billigst saavel over **Hamborg** som **England**
til **AMERIKA & AUSTRALIEN.**

**Med
store
Damp-
skibe.**

**Lave
Priser.**

God Kost.

**Ingen
Ophold.**

Største Bekvemmelighed. Udmærket Behandling.

MÆRK! Kjøb ikke Billet før De har
hørt Passageprisen paa mit
Kontor. Det er til Deres
egen Fordeel!

R. H. REEH,
2, Toldbodgade 2, Hj. af Nyhavn.
Indgang i Toldbodgade.
KJØBENHAVN. K.

An emigration agent's business card in the 1880's.

Mormon Emigration

A very effective type of emigration agent was the Mormon missionary. Mormons came to Europe in the mid-1800's, and they had good success with their missionary efforts, especially in England and Scandinavia. Conversion was accompanied by strong encouragement to move to the Mormon paradise of Zion. This was in Utah, near the Great Salt Lake. The Mormons themselves arranged the journey and all expenses. More details of the Mormon emigration are discussed in the volume, *America Fever*, in this series on *The Dream of America*.

The Mormon route to Utah

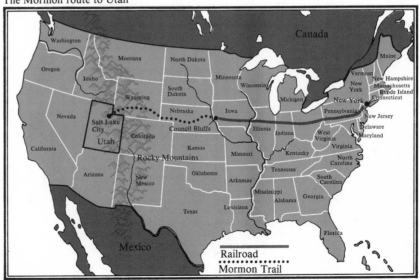

agreed that the price of a ticket to New York should be set at a certain amount, or that a certain ceiling should be set on fees. If someone broke the agreement, he had to pay a fine into a common fund. These agreements never lasted more than a few months. Then somebody disobeyed the rules and refused to pay the fine. But the general agents were able to agree on some things. In Copenhagen, they established a pension fund for themselves. As far as is known, this pension fund functioned without any problems.

A fund was established in Salt Lake City. Poor Mormons from Europe could borrow money for their journey to Utah and pay it back when they arrived. The money was loaned at interest, so the travel fund grew from $5,000 in 1850 to $1,000,000 in 1877. Mormon missionaries acted as their own general agents. The converts were not to travel to America by ordinary means. When a few hundred new converts were ready, the missionaries would charter a whole steamship from Liverpool. Mormons from all parts of Europe came together and sailed from Liverpool to New York. Under the leadership of the missionaries, with hymn singing and readings from Scripture, thousands of emigrants started the long journey to the distant state beyond the mountains.

In the years before the transcontinental railroad was finished in 1869, this long journey to Salt Lake City was a difficult one. It usually took three or four months. Many died on the way. Others lost their faith before they got to Utah. A settlement was established in Nebraska, for example, by a group of Danish immigrants who had drifted away from the Mormon religion during their long journey to Zion.

The Mormons headed for Salt Lake City. They had to travel on foot before the railroad came in 1869. For some 1,200 miles, they pushed a hand cart with all their belongings. Here is a bill for "three hand cart shares," signed in 1860 by Johan Stenstrom (2 shares) and Christian Christensen (1 share).

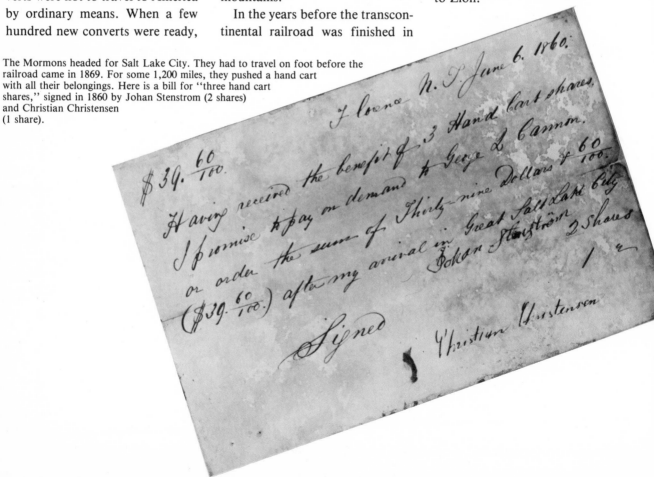

Trails crossed the prairie, and the immigrants could follow them in their prairie schooners as they moved westwards, looking for land to settle on and farm.

The Union Pacific and Central Pacific railroad stretched from coast to coast after 1869. This is the bridge across Devil's Gate in Utah.

Direct Ties with Northern Europe

Baltic Lloyd

The tragic Ottawa Affair in 1866, discussed on pages 28-29, had discouraged direct lines from Scandinavia to America. But already in 1869, a new direct line was established from Copenhagen to New York. Danish and German capital was invested in equal shares. The line was called Baltic Lloyd, and it was a success until 1874. At that time, emigration decreased temporarily, and the line was forced to go out of business.

About 12,000 Scandinavians emigrated with Baltic Lloyd, two thirds of them Swedes and the rest Danes. The direct route was by far the easiest way to travel, but it was also more expensive. Most emigrants still went by way of Hamburg or Liverpool. During the years 1874-1879, there was no direct passenger route from Scandinavia to America.

In the years following, Denmark became the leading Scandinavian country in the direct transportation of emigrants to America. Until as late as 1909, the only direct line from Scandinavia to New York was in Danish hands.

Accidents and Shipwrecks

Around the year 1879, emigration from Scandinavia began to increase. Danish businessmen saw an opportunity. They founded a new passenger line in 1879 and bought a ship, "Thingvalla." They called their line the Thingvalla Line. It

Thingvalla Line's ship, "Danmark," had to be deserted in mid-Atlantic in 1889.

was a great success in the first years. It got more emigrants from Denmark and southern Sweden than any of the German or English lines.

But little by little, the company ran into problems in competition with the big international passenger lines. Furthermore, its ships were hit by a number of disasters over the years.

The first one happened in 1883, when the "Hekla" went down in Oslo fjord.

Much more serious and strange was the accident that happened in August, 1888. Two of the company's ships, "Thingvalla" and "Geiser," were passing each other in clear weather, yet they crashed into each other. The force was so great that "Geiser" sank in five minutes with most of its 79 passengers and the crew. "Thingvalla" was on its way to New York with 455 passengers. It received a gaping hole in its bow but miraculously reached Halifax. The accident was surrounded by some mystery. Considering the huge size of the Atlantic Ocean, it was unbelievable that two ships from the same country and company would meet on the high seas and actually crash into each other.

"Geiser" and "Thingvalla" hit each other because the officer in charge of one of the ships became panic stricken as the two ships approached one another. They were both sailing on the same sea lane. The officer was not completely sure of the rules at sea. The rule is that ships pass to the left of each other. When he panicked, he sailed his ship right into the other one.

The second mate on the "Geiser" told this tale of how he survived the collision: "I was asleep in my bunk when I was awakened by a terrible crash. I opened my eyes to see the bow of a

The "Thingvalla" after her collision with "Geiser" in 1888. The gaping hole in the bow was the result. It seems almost miraculous that the ship could make port safely in that condition.

steamship plowing its way through my cabin. It splintered planks and boards like toothpicks. My first thought was that the only way I could save myself was to jump on board the other steamer. To stay where I was meant to be crushed or drowned. Our ship soon began to sink, so I had little time. I jumped out of my bunk. When I set foot on the floor, I saw the anchor chain of the other ship, right in front of me. And when the ship pulled away from 'Geiser,' I got on board and was saved."

That kind of accident does not inspire much confidence on the part of emigrants when they are choosing the line they want to sail with. The accident almost wiped out the company financially. And the situation became worse when the company's new passenger ship, "Danmark," had to be abandoned in the middle of the Atlantic because of mechanical difficulties that could not be repaired. The propeller axle broke and knocked a hole in the hull. The ship began to sink slowly with 800 emigrants and 100 crewmen on board. A small freighter with room for twenty passengers came to the rescue. It took all 900 people on board and sailed with them to the Azores while the "Danmark" slowly disappeared under the waves.

A few years later, "Thingvalla" crashed into an iceberg. The ship was badly shaken, but it did not go down. However, the public finally lost all confidence in the Thingvalla Line, and it was forced to go out of business.

The company was taken over by a new Danish steamship line, DFDS. This new line set out to prove that it could run a safe passenger service across the Atlantic. It changed its name to the Scandinavian-American Line. But the public was slow to put much confidence in the new line.

The next accident was worse than any of the earlier ones.

In July, 1904, one of the Scandinavian-American Line's older ships, "Norge," hit Rockall Islet, west of Scotland. There were 773 people on board, and only 146

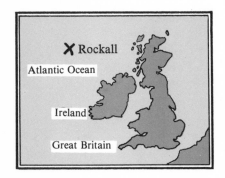

Rockall Islet

Christian Mølsted was the artist who painted this reconstructed view of the wreck of the "Norge" in July, 1904.

were rescued. A total of 627 people drowned.

It was a terrible accident. One of the survivors described it as follows, "From the lifeboat, we saw 'Norge' go down. The captain stood on the bridge, and along the railing stood the passengers, pale as death from fear. They screamed no more. It was as if Death had paralyzed them. Now and then, a man or woman threw themselves madly into the ocean. They bobbed in the water for a moment and then disappeared. Suddenly 'Norge' raised on end. Those on board rolled down the deck and disappeared into the ocean, while their horrible screams sounded like the howls of wild animals. For a moment, 'Norge' stood upright out of the water. Then suddenly she went under, sending two great columns of water high into the air."

Even though ships had become larger and the engines more powerful, it was still dangerous to cross the Atlantic. The many people who made the crossing still had to hope and pray that they would have a successful crossing.

An Emigration Agent's Correspondence

Could an agent sit back and wait for emigrants to come in on their own? Was it necessary for him to tempt them in some way so that they would buy tickets to America? How did an agent make contact with the people who wanted to emigrate?

To a certain extent, emigrants probably came on their own. Somehow or another, they heard or read something about America. Maybe a letter from a relative had been read aloud among friends. They might have seen articles about America in some newspaper.

In time, people might get the idea that they wanted to emigrate and then simply come into the emigration agent's office.

A large percentage of the population of Europe, especially young people between the ages of 18 and 28, were seriously considering emigration in those years.

Letters from friends and relatives in America were very important means of persuading others to emigrate.

The owner of this inn in Aalborg, Denmark, was also an emigration agent for two English lines around 1900.

By far the most common questions were about ticket prices and conditions in America. The cost of the ticket was very important to the emigrants. They were poor people. It might be difficult for them to raise $20, which was the normal price for a ticket from Sweden to New York at that time.

The other big question was about conditions in America. It is interesting that the number of questions about America fell dramatically by 1888. This is probably connected with the fact that a lot of people had already emigrated during the 1880's. More than 40,000 Swedes came to America in the single year of 1884. These people now wrote home and told the others where they should come in America, and what conditions were like. So the destination of these later emigrants was already decided and they did not need to ask the ticket agent about things like that.

Letters of Inquiry

A Swedish emigration agent's correspondence from the 1880's has been saved till the present. In the mid-1950's, a collection of old letters was found in a barn near Gothenburg, Sweden. It turned out to be a complete collection of the correspondence of two brothers named Larsson who were emigration agents. They worked for a small English company, the Guion Line. This collection of correspondence reveals how many letters an agent received every year, with questions about ticket prices and where to go in America. The office of the Larsson brothers received 12,000 to 15,000 letters a year during the 1880's.

The letters reveal the kinds of questions people asked. Their most common questions are shown below.

Question	1882-1884	1888
1. About ticket prices	31.0%	44.3%
2. About ships and conditions on board	4.4%	6.3%
3. About documents needed, especially for draft age men	1.3%	8.7%
4. Information about America	48.8%	20.3%
5. About possibilities for jobs or buying land in America	5.2%	0.3%

Draft Dodgers

A few people in 1882-1884 asked about the papers and documents that were needed in order to emigrate. More people asked the same question in 1888. This was connected with a change in Swedish law in 1887. Men had to show the police a document proving that they had already completed their compulsory military training. Young men would not be allowed to emigrate just before they were due to be drafted. The result of this was that Swedish emigration by way of Copenhagen increased rapidly. Young Swedish men traveled first to Denmark, and from there, they skipped off to America. Danish agents advertised the Copenhagen route in all the Swedish newspapers. "Discharge certificate not needed," they advertised in big letters. Therefore, Swedish draft dodgers streamed into Copenhagen.

The Swedish government complained many times to the Danish government that Danish emigration agents were encouraging Swedish soldiers to desert. Nothing was done about it by the authorities in Denmark. It was not their problem, it was a Swedish problem. In Denmark, they looked upon this stream of draft dodgers as a good source of income.

Arbeidslønninger i de Nordamerikanske Fristater.

For Mænd.

		fra doll.	fra cents	til doll.	til cents
Bagere	Maaned	50	.	75	.
Barberere	Uge	6	.	12	.
Billedskjærere	Maaned	50	.	70	.
Blyhvidtsfabrikanter	Dag	1	75	3	.
Bogbindere	—	1	75	3	.
Bryggere	Uge	10	.	15	.
Bygningsarbeidere	Dag	2	.	4	.
Brøndgravere	—	2	.	3	.
Bødkere	—	1	75	3	.
Bøssemagere	—	1	75	3	.
Cigarmagere	—	2	.	4	.
Dagleiere i By og paa Land, med Kost	Maaned	15	.	24	.
Dampmaskinearbeidere	Dag	3	.	4	.
Fotografer	Maaned	45	.	75	.
Farvere	—	30	.	40	.
Forgyldere	Dag	2	.	3	.
Gasarbeidere	—	2	.	3	.
Gibsformere	—	1	75	3	.
Glarmestere	—	1	50	3	.
Gravører	—	1	50	3	.
Handelsbetjente	Uge	8	.	21	.
Hattemagere	Dag	2	.	3	50
Hjulmagere	Maaned	40	.	55	.
Jernstøbere	Dag	2	.	4	.
Kammagere	Uge	5	.	10	.
Kurvemagere	—	8	.	13	.

		fra doll.	cents	til doll.	cents
Knapmagere	Dag	2	•	3	50
Konditore med Kost	Maaned	25	•	30	•
Kobbersmede	Dag	2	•	3	•
Kudske	Uge	8	•	16	•
— Omnibus	Dag	1	75	2	50
Lysestøbere	Uge	8	•	10	•
Lærlinge	—	2	50	6	•
Maskinbyggere	Dag	2	•	4	•
Metalarbeidere	—	2	•	4	•
Meiselfabrikanter	—	2	•	3	50
Murere	—	1	75	4	•
Malere	—	1	75	4	•
—	Uge	10	•	16	•
Møllere	Maaned	50	•	75	•
Møllebyggere	—	50	•	70	•
Omnibus-Conductører	Dag	2	•		
Opvartere, med Kost	Maaned	15	•	30	•
Pakhuskarle	Uge	9	•	15	•
Pottemagere	Dag	1	75	3	•
Papirmagere	Dag	1	50	2	25
Polerere	Uge	7	•	12	•
Politibetjente	Aar	1000	•		
Remmefabrikanter	Dag	2	•	2	75
Rebslagere	—	2	50	3	50
Sadelmagere	—	1	75	3	50
Seilmagere	—	1	75	3	75
Sølvarbeidere	Maaned	40	•	60	•
Skiferdækkere	Dag	2	•	3	•
Skomagere	—	1	25	3	•
Skrædere	—	1	50	4	50
Skiltefabrikanter	Uge	10	•	18	•
Smed, Anker-	Maaned	60	•	70	•
— Grov-	Dag	2	•	4	•
— Pengekiste-	Uge	15	•	22	•
— Klein-	—	12	•	20	•
— Kniv-	Maaned	40	•	65	•
— Nagel-	Dag	4	•	5	•

		fra doll.	cents	til doll.	cents
Skjærslibere	Dag	1	75	4	•
Snedkere	—	1	75	3	•
Steenhuggere	—	2	•	3	75
Sættere, pr. 1000 Bog-staver		•	35	•	50
Tagtækkere	Dag	1	75	3	•
Tapetserere	—	1	75	3	•
Tømmermænd, Hus-	—	1	75	3	•
— Skibs-	—	2	•	3	50
Trykkeriarbeidere	Uge	10	•	20	•
Uhrmagere	Dag	2	•	3	50

For Fruentimmer.

		fra doll.	cents	til doll.	cents
Barnepiger med Kost	Uge	1	50	2	50
Bogfalsere	—	3	•	8	•
Bogheftere	Dag	•	75	1	•
Stuepige med Kost	Uge	1	50	4	•
Damefrisørinde	—	4	50	7	50
Kjøkkenpige med Kost	—	2	50	8	•
Lærerinde	—	5	•	12	•
Medhjælperske hos Hatte-magere		3	50	7	•
Ved Blomsterfabriker	—	1	50	5	•
- Broderi	—	4	•	8	•
Buxesyere	Par	•	40	2	50
Handskesyerske	Uge	3	50	5	•
Kappesyerske	—	•	60	2	60
Krinolinesyerske	—	3	50	4	•
Andre Arbeider, hvorved Fruentimmer i Almin-delighed beskjæftiges	—	2 à 6	•	6 à 10	•

From a handbook for emigrants published in 1871. Many such handbooks were published in the years before 1914. These pages show wages for different jobs in the USA. For example, a cigar maker could earn from $2 to $4 a day. A chambermaid (**Stuepige**) could earn $1.50 to $4 a week plus room and board.

Subagents

The general agents in a major European city were of various types. In Copenhagen, for example, some represented the English lines, others the German lines. There were also representatives for a large firm in Hamburg, Morris & Co., that sent emigrants from Hamburg to England, where they sailed from Liverpool to New York on English ships. Finally, there was the main agency of the Danish Thingvalla Line and its successors.

All the general agents competed with each other. They had to sell the voyage to America like other businessmen sell other products. Therefore, a network to sell tickets all over the country was absolutely necessary.

Previous to the Emigration Law of 1868, for example, the Copenhagen general agents already had their subagents certified in the little kingdom of Denmark in 1868. We can imagine how many there were spread over the whole continent of Europe. In the years to come, stiffer competition led to a rapid increase in the number of subagents. By 1878, there were 571 in Denmark. Other countries saw a similar increase in number. Every general agent had about fifty subagents. By 1886, the number in Denmark and other countries had almost doubled again. All of these agents and subagents sold "America voyages," that is, one way tickets to New York and other North American ports.

Being an emigration clerk, as the subagents were sometimes called,

Aarhus, Denmark, in 1907. The hotel on the corner is also the office of an emigration subagent.

could be a part-time job for a craftsman, innkeeper or shopkeeper. Shoemakers and bartenders were often subagents. They had a big poster or metal sign outside their door. There were pictures of impressive ships with many sails and with smoke stacks billowing smoke. Inside, there were stacks of pamphlets, descriptions of ships, maps of America and Australia, and similar literature. Furthermore, the shoemaker or innkeeper was usually a good talker who could make it all come alive for his customers.

A good deal of information about America was circulated by means of these subagents. The printed matter they passed out came mostly from American railroads or other companies that wanted to sell land. It also came from factories or mining companies that wanted workers. The passenger lines sent these pamphlets to Europe free of charge. The general agents distributed them to the subagents. This happened all over Europe, from the western coast of Ireland to the inland Russian steppes. The pam-

Vejviser

til

Union Pacific Jernbanens Land.

12 Millioner Acres

af det bedste Farm og Mineral Land i Amerika

tilsalgs af

Union Pacific Jernbane Compagniet,

i Landstykker efter Kjøbernes Ønske og til billige Priser.

Omaha, Nebra[...]

Land-Departemen[...]
Union Pacific Jernbanebygning, Hjørnet

1870.

TOLK OG VEILEDER

FOR

SKANDINAVISKE UDVANDRERE

PAA REISEN
TIL OG IGJENNEM AMERIKA.

En letfattelig og nyttig Lærebog i det engelske Sprog.

Udarbeidet efter mange Aars Ophold i Amerika

af

William K. Gundersen,
Kongelig Translateur og Tolk i Engelsk

Kjøbenhavn.
Hos Axel E. Aamodt.
S. Triers Bogtrykkeri.

One of the many guidebooks for emigrants, this one published in 1871.

The American government stimulated railroad construction by giving the companies tracts of land along their right-of-way. The railroad companies then sold the land to settlers in units the size of an individual family farm. American railroads also advertised in Europe to sell their vast tracts of land.

phlets were printed in dozens of languages so that the people throughout Europe could read about America in their own language.

The clever subagent did not waste his speeches or pamphlets on just anyone. He concentrated on those who could be convinced to emigrate. These were often the strong young men and women who worked on farms for low wages. Or they were poor families with an unemployed father, or craftsmen who had been put out of work by cheap mass produced goods. These were the people the subagent was interested in.

He made a very high fee on every ticket. If he could sell tickets to a whole family or group of young men and women, he could earn more on emigration than on his main business. Selling three adult tickets gave him more money than a farm laborer could earn in a month of hard work.

There were many areas where emigration was high—but was emigration high because the agents were persuasive, or was it just because a lot of people wanted to emigrate? This is a difficult question to answer.

The Yankee System

The network of subagents was very important as a source of information about emigration. But the subagents were really not terribly good at selling tickets. By themselves, they could hardly have gotten the rate of emigration to increase as sharply as it did. Maybe this was because they had not been to America themselves. They could tell about the wonderful farm land in Nebraska, but they had never actually seen it. It was hard to know if you could really depend on what they said.

Returning Emigrants

The general agents had another sales system in addition to the subagents. It was even more effective, although it had to work a bit less openly because its agents were not licensed by the authorities. This was the so-called "Yankee" system. Emigrants who had come back to their native land were sent from house to house. Their appearance alone was proof that a person could strike it rich in America. Their fancy hats, cigars and golden watch chains, and their rolling American accent impressed the people back home in the Old Country. These returning emigrants were called Yankees.

The Yankee system developed into a regular business. It became a vast international network. The passenger lines did not have many passengers on the return from

The returning emigrant or Yankee with his pockets full of dollars. Swedish drawing from 1904.

America to Europe. Because they had plenty of room, it cost them almost nothing to bring a few emigrants back to Europe for free. Then the line could use them in the work of providing more emigrants for the return voyage to America.

It was also nice for the new Americans to get a free trip back to their native land. They could even earn a little money while they were home, just as the subagents could, by selling tickets to America. The Yankees generally came home to their native country in the autumn. During the winter, each of them gathered a group of emigrants whom they then accompanied back to America the following spring.

Newspapers of the 1880's have many advertisements by these Yankees. They offered their services as travel leaders for emigrants. Many people were afraid to emigrate because they did not know the English language. They were afraid that they would be cheated and misled by everyone they met. But they felt safe in the company of a fellow countryman.

The Yankees often took off with large groups of between 50 and 150 new emigrants. The money invested by the passenger lines in the Yankee system came back with handsome dividends.

It was not just the passenger lines that used Yankees. American railroad companies used them, too, to sell land or to recruit workers.

The Yankees could earn extra money by playing off one agent against another. The agent who gave him the most money per ticket could win the business of his whole group. For example, here is a letter from the general agent for the Hamburg-America Line in Copenhagen. He is writing to one of his subagents. The letter shows how general agents competed for the travel groups assembled by Yankees.

"March 14, 1884

"Mr. R. P. Jensen
"Pedersgave
"Sindal, Jutland
"Denmark

"You inquire about travel arrangements for the two returned Americans. As you know, I have to have 65 crowns for Hamburg-New York, so you must find out how much the Americans want in cash. Add that to the 65 crowns,

Advertisement for English lessons, taught by a man who had "lived in North and South America for many years."

and then also add on your own fee. The total will be the price a passenger must pay for the tickets to New York. For example, if the Americans want 15 crowns and you want 5 crowns, and I must have 65 crowns, then the price is 85 crowns to New York and 135

A Yankee trying to convince a family to travel to America with him.

crowns to Chicago. Furthermore, I offer each American a free ticket from Hamburg to New York if he brings along at least ten adults for the voyage, that means a ticket for an extra good cabin with extra service. I have an American with a large group from Odense on March 29, and we have arranged the trip in the aforementioned way."

Who Made Money on the Voyage to America?

This Yankee was really getting good terms. He was earning three times as much as the official subagent. Let us say the subagent was sending a group of 100 emigrants. All together, they would pay 8,500 crowns for the voyage to New York. The money would then presumably be divided like this:

65

1. The Hamburg-America Line, to cover the costs of transportation, etc.

4,500 crowns

2. Transportation to Hamburg @ 10 crowns per emigrant

1,000 crowns

3. Income for the general agent

1,000 crowns

4. Income for the subagent

500 crowns

5. Income for the Yankee

1,500 crowns

Total   8,500 crowns

The Hamburg-America Line had the tremendous expenses of maintaining and building ocean liners, providing food and service to the passengers on the voyage, maintaining their head office and those of general agents throughout Europe, advertising in several countries, and more besides. Yet they only got about half of what the emigrants paid for their tickets. Of the remainder, 35% went to various agents. No wonder the passenger lines had a tight budget and worked hard to hold down the fees they paid to agents.

A lot of money was involved in emigration. In 1882, a year of heavy emigration, $210,000 was paid for passenger tickets from Denmark to America. That was only a small percentage of the total

Stam-

Løbe-Nummer.	Af hvilket Sogn ind-lagt.	Stam-Nummer.	Fulde Navn.	Alder.	Fødested.	Sidste Opholdssted.	Om straffet.
245	Birkerød	30	Ulrik Christian T......	26 8/10 69	Usserød.	Ladegaarden Kjøbenhavn	2×5 5×6 } Dages Vand og Brød.
249	Karlebo	98	Bendt A....	49	Gjentofte	Hørsholm	Nei
324	Birkerød	4	Christian Peter H......	11 4/6 72	Birkerød	Birkerød	Nei
400	Karlebo	14	Marie Florentine Jørgine H.....	1 5/12 75	Brøns-holmsdal	—	—

bog.

Været paa Anstalten.			Føde.		Flids-godt-gjørelse.		Klæder.		Udført Arbeide til Værdi.		Skyldig.		Tilgode.		
Fra	Til	Antal Dage	Kr.	Ø.	Kr.	Ø.	Kr.	Ø.	Kr.	Ø.	Kr.	Ø.	Kr.	Ø.	
²/₉69	⁸/₅70	249	69	63	4	37	253	22¹)	34	16	293	6			¹) Inclusive Reiseomkost. til Amerika hvortil han er sendt.
¹⁰/₁₁70	³¹/₃71	142	37	45	8	4	7	66	62	20			9	5	Absenteret sig.
²/₁₀71	³¹/₁₂71	91	25	59			11	58			37	17			Confirmeret ²/₁₀75 og an-bragt i Smedelære hos Smed S. i B. den ⁵/₁₂75.
¹/₁72	³¹/₁₂72	366	106	75			24	75			131	50			
¹/₁73	³¹/₁₂73	365	114	6			29	"			143	6			
¹/₁74	³¹/₁₂74	365	121	67			17	33			139	"			
¹/₁75	⁵/₁₂75	338	121	68			75	8			196	76			
		1525	489	75			157	74			647	49			
⁵/₁₂71	³¹/₁₂74	27	9	"							9	"			
¹/₁75	³¹/₁₂75	365	131	40			25	28			156	68			
¹/₁76															

of all European emigration. By way of comparison, the total budget of the Danish government that year was only $7,000,000. Furthermore, emigrants took money with them. In some cases, they took a small fortune. Emigration was a big economic loss for the countries of Europe. The loss was even greater when you consider the loss of workers that was involved.

The many opportunities to make money by finding new emigrants probably helped to increase the number of emigrants. But one thing that bothered the authorities and a lot of ordinary citizens was this: What kind of an impression did all these agents and Yankees give of America? An unscrupulous agent could give a completely false impression on the country they were sending people to.

It was to avoid this, among other things, that European countries passed emigration laws. But did these laws really work? It was impossible for the authorities to control the agents in their hunt for new emigrants. Even when the Yankee system was prohibited by

European countries could get rid of poor people and criminals by sending them to America. Here is one example. In 1876, the Danish authorities released Ulrik Christian T..., no. 245, a hardened criminal, and paid his expenses to go to America.

law, it could not be controlled. And when the police tried to step in, the agent always found loopholes in the law.

Exporting People With Problems

Some people considered mass emigration to be of benefit to society. It afforded an opportunity to get rid of people with problems. Why discourage them from leaving? And if their problems turned out to be even worse in America than at home—so what? Then it was somebody else's problem.

It was precisely this point of view that led one general agent to write a letter to every parish council in the kingdom of Denmark, some two thousand in all, suggesting that he could help them solve their welfare problems by quietly sending the poor to America. The ticket only cost 100 crowns, once and for all. That was considerably cheaper than supporting people on welfare all their lives. Who knows how many parish councils accepted offers like this? We know for a fact that it was done. Thousands of cases are known from many parts of Europe. In England, 339,000 individuals on welfare were sent to other countries in the twenty year period, 1849-1869. Part of the money was raised from private sources, and the people on welfare had to pay a small amount themselves. Most of them went to Australia or New Zealand, but many ended in America, too.

America Becomes Aware of the Influence of Agents

Officials in America started to worry about the situation in the 1880's, when the stream of immigrants swelled to over half a million every year. Congress established a commission in 1891 to investigate the background for this flood of emigrants. Members of the commission visited Europe. They seemed to have realized the influence of agents for the passenger lines. In one of their reports to Congress, the commission wrote, "It is their business to bring as many people to America as possible. They travel through the European countries with their agents, sending off anyone who can raise the money for a ticket."

They realized the influence of the agents. A major part of a later report to Congress was devoted to proving that the wave of Russian emigrants after 1900 had been stimulated by agents for the passenger lines. These agents travelled throughout Russia and eastern Europe in order to find emigrants. Whether or not too much was made of this for political reasons is hard to say. But that it actually did occur is undeniable. In 1898, for example, the Scandinavian-American Line made it one of its goals to "capture" Finland. Until 1900, there had been very little emigration from Finland. Suddenly, a wave of emigration started from Finland. This was at the same time as Russia's emigration boom.

Advertisement by the general agent for State Line in a Norwegian language newspaper published in Minneapolis.

Russian emigrants around 1900.

The Emigrants

52 Million New Lives

Fifty-two million emigrants were on their way to a new life. They were the ones who decided to emigrate. It was a very big decision in every one of their lives.

They thought hard before they made the decision to emigrate. But there did not need to be as many decisions as there were individual emigrants. About half of them just followed along. Often the father made the decision. The wife and children followed along. The wife was often the least happy to leave her homeland and family. Were men more adventurous, or less tied to the homeland, or was it just because they were the ones who decided?

A few examples can show how it happened with individual families.

Those Who Never Left

Niels Jensen Nielsen owned a small farm near Givskud in Denmark. He could hardly support his large family. One of his children later wrote about how the decision to emigrate was handled in this family. "It finally came to heated arguments between my parents. Father was sick and tired of a cottager's life. He wanted to emi-

Leaving home. Emigrants from Smaland in Sweden, ready to leave, around 1900.

Before railroads, overland transportation in Europe was by stagecoach or wagon.

grate. But Mother, knowing the Nielsen family's weakness for the bottle, was afraid of going to a strange country. She might end up alone and having to support herself and their many children. But when Grandfather died, she finally let herself be talked into leaving. The little cottage and all that we owned were sold, tickets were purchased, and Mother reluctantly began the journey. The first stop was the neighboring town of Vejle, and the family went no farther. They were met by the agent who had sold them the tickets. He explained that their places had already been sold to somebody else. There had been a mixup between subagents in two different towns. We had to wait for the next ship. Of course, Father was angry. Here he was with his family and a few belongings in a little town where he now had to find a place to stay for several weeks. Mother stepped in and took advantage of the situation to convince Father to change his mind. He told the agent to get out. The money for the tickets was refunded, and our family settled in Vejle.''

The wife got her way. There was a question of whether or not this was the right decision. The husband remained bitter for the rest of his life. His wife had stopped him from achieving the possibilities that America would have offered.

Children Decide

In another case, it was the children, and not the parents, who made the decision for the whole family. A family of farm laborers in Møn were visited by a Yankee. He had originally emigrated from their area. His descriptions of America made no great impression on the parents, but they did on the

71

children. They announced the next morning that they would all emigrate as soon as they were of age. The parents would eventually be left alone. Faced with this prospect, the father and mother made the same decision and emigrated as a family with their children.

The Auction

Those who wanted to could not always emigrate. A common laborer would have a very hard time scraping together the money. They often had to sell everything they owned in order to raise money for the ticket. Auction records from the 1880's show how the emigrants sold house and home, clothing and furniture, before they left.

A table was set up outside the house. All the household possessions were brought outside: furniture, linens, pots and pans, and everything else. These things were displayed to the crowd and sold to the highest bidder. It must have been strange for the family to see their possessions sold off at low prices. Finally, the house was sold. The family now had some money, and a few boxes and bundles of goods that they planned to take along. The ties with their homeland were being broken.

Even before the auction, the father had signed a ticket contract with an emigration agent. Now they were anxious to see whether the auction had brought in enough money to pay for the tickets.

Departure and Voyage

Then came the difficult time to say good-bye to friends and relatives, and to look for the last time at the old familiar sights, woods, fields, birds and houses. They were now travelling by wagon, by train, or by boat to the big city. In the city, they were met by the emigration runners (see page 46). After a few days in the city, the family would sail across the North Sea to Hull in England. This was often the worst part of the voyage. The ships were small and crowded. Food was not included in the price. The emigrants had to bring their own sausages, bread, butter, and the like. It could be awful on the crowded ship because the North Sea waters can be very rough and the ships were small.

The night in Hull was spent in ramshackle buildings or bad hotels, and the next day, the train took them across England to Liverpool. There the family might have to wait several days before the real ocean voyage began.

Copenhagen harbor in 1875. The ships to America left from here.

Castle Garden was built in 1807. First it was a fort, then a circus, and beginning in 1855, it was the place of entry for immigrants. All kinds of agents hung around outside. This picture shows soldiers recruiting immigrants into the Union Army during the Civil War, 1861-1865.

The voyage across the Atlantic has been described in earlier chapters. Excitement on board the big ships was great. After about a week on the open sea, the ship approached New York, came in sight of the Statue of Liberty, and docked at Castle Garden at the lower tip of Manhattan. This was an old building through which millions of European immigrants passed into the promised land.

Arrival in New York

About half of the passengers who landed in New York did not have tickets to go any farther. They stepped out of Castle Garden and counted on their good luck to get along in the confusion of New York. Outside of Castle Garden was a big crowd of agents, day and night. They tried to lure the emigrants into all kinds of things. Some were agents for railroad

How the immigrants moved westwards after their arrival in New York.

companies, land companies, industries or mining companies that were looking for workers. There was also a large number of agents who wanted to exchange money, help with the luggage, or get the immigrants to stay at a certain hotel. Some were there to cheat the immigrants in any way they could. Fortunately, some of the immigrants were met by relatives who had immigrated earlier, or were led through the crowd of agents by a Yankee who was the leader of their group.

These newly arrived immigrants were still pale from seasickness. They wore wrinkled clothing. Most of them knew nothing about the country they were in, and they spoke little or no English. But they were worth a fortune nonetheless. Their manpower could carry on the growth of America. The tremendous economic expansion of America in the late nineteenth century was connected with the cultivation of the prairie, the planting of wheat, and the development and mechanization of industry. Of course, the agents hanging around Castle Garden did not worry about all that. But they knew that they could make some money by providing immigrants to the people who needed them.

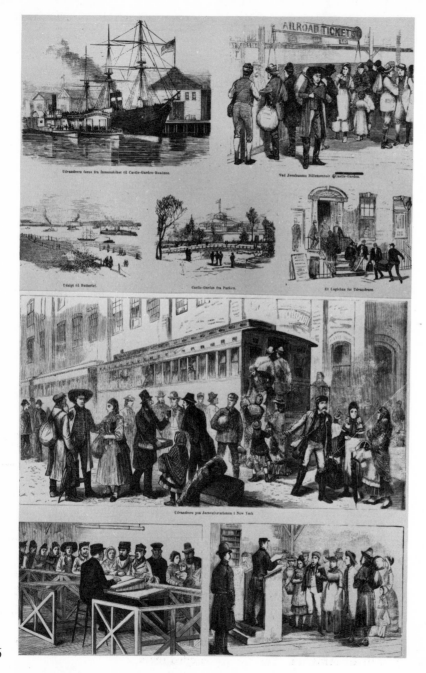

From the immigrant ship to the final destination could be time consuming and difficult. It might take several days to get through Castle Garden and get a railroad ticket out of New York.

A letter from a railroad executive in Minnesota during the 1870's shows how they fought to get immigrants: "We cannot compete with the other railroad companies in securing foreign immigrants who come through Castle Garden. We have to pay just as much as the others pay. All the officials at Castle Garden are paid by one or another railroad. The company that bids the highest gets the most immigrant workers."

Almost all guidebooks for emigrants warned against talking to the agents that swarmed around both outside and inside Castle Garden in New York. Most of them were only out to swindle the immigrants. A wise immigrant, who had still not decided where he wanted to go after arriving in New York, would go to an employment agency for a job. There were many of them in New York. They were all private agencies, and many of them were run by the passenger lines. There were no public employment agencies in those days.

Over half of the immigrants arriving in New York, however, already had a ticket to some specific destination outside the city. This might be another city on the eastern coast, a farm on the prairie where friends or relatives lived, or a factory that had promised a good job. Maybe the tales of gold in California and the mountains of the west lured them across the continent.

Railroads and the Immigrants

It was still hard to travel around in Europe during the last half of the 1860's. But at that very time, a great network for travel was being developed between the two continents of Europe and America. In the smallest village in Germany or Italy, people could buy a ticket to another tiny village or frontier community in distant Wisconsin or California.

For the American railroads, it was important to attract people

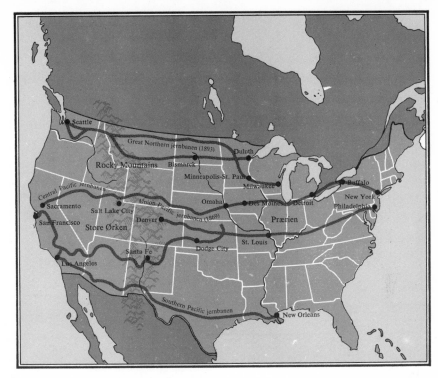

The first transcontinental railroads in America.

American steam locomotive, 1867.

77

from Europe, first of all to have workers to build the railroad, and later, to have inhabitants in the areas served by the railroad.

The American government gave some of the railroads alternate sections of land along the railroad's right-of-way. This was empty prairie land for the most part. The railroads sold it to farmers in units of 160 acres. When this land finally came under cultivation, there would be wheat or corn or livestock to be sent to market. They were sent on the railroad. Likewise, when supplies and machinery were needed on the farms, they came by railroad. When the land was settled, the railroads really began to serve their purpose, and they began to make money.

Immigrants did not decide on their own to move into the empty prairie states of the west. Immigrants had to be attracted inland. All of the railroad companies, large and small, sent their agents to New York in order to recruit immigrants. But the competition was ferocious. Soon many companies began to make contacts on the other side of the Atlantic. Railroads often worked hand in hand with a passenger line. The passenger line used its network of agents to sell tickets on a particular railroad. They tried to provide immigrants for the parts of America served by their railroad.

Advertisements in American foreign language newspapers for the sale of uncultivated prairie land. It was usually offered in blocks of 160 acres.

When an agent in Norway, for example, was asked which part of America he would recommend, then he would always send people to that part of Wisconsin, Minnesota or North Dakota where he had contacts with an American railroad company. The railroads paid a commission of 10% on every ticket sold in Europe, 5% to the passenger line and 5% to the agent. Furthermore, the railroad provided the agent with free literature, posters, maps and pamphlets. The railroad lands were described in glowing terms. Thousands of copies of this type of literature, printed in many European languages, were sent across the Atlantic and passed out by subagents.

There was a lot of money behind the railroads. In order to assure that they got enough immigrants for their lands, the railroads began in the 1880's to buy French, German and English passenger lines. They wanted to assure themselves a profit on the transportation of immigrants, and at the same time, they wanted to establish a direct contact with the people of Europe through their own network of agents and subagents.

First class accommodations on American railroads were elegant in the Victorian era. This drawing is from 1875.

From New York to Nebraska by train in the 1880's took about eight days. It was hard to get much sleep on the train if you were not travelling first class, and most of the immigrants were not.

Canada also recruited immigrants in this way after confederation united the country in 1867. A transcontinental railroad was built by the Canadian Pacific Railway. Around the year 1900, when Canada was making an all-out effort to get people to settle the vast prairie provinces of Saskatchewan and Alberta, the Canadian railroad purchased the big British passenger line, the Allan Line. A major recruiting campaign was launched in 1900 through the Allan Line's agents in northern Europe. Many Scandinavians and Germans Canadian Pacific Railway finished its transcontinental line in November, 1885. This meant that the prairie lands of Saskatchewan and Alberta were opened for settlement by European immigrants.

emigrated as a result and ended their days as farmers in Canada.

The railroads also used other methods to attract settlers. When the Northern Pacific wanted immigrants to settle in Minnesota in the 1870's, representatives of the railroad traveled around to the immigrant communities of Minnesota. They gave away free stationery, envelopes and stamps to the settlers, and they asked them to write to friends and relatives in their native country. They were to urge them to come to Minnesota.

It cost more, but it was better to send a few selected immigrants to Europe. There they could function as Yankees for the railroads.

Prepaid Tickets

Atlantic passenger lines had their networks of agents in Europe, but they also had similar networks in America. The work of these American agents and subagents was to sell prepaid tickets. Prepaid tickets could be purchased in America by immigrants and sent to Europe for use by family and friends.

Wages were much higher in America than in Europe. An ordinary worker could quickly earn enough money to buy a ticket for other members of his family. He could do it much faster than a worker in Europe.

Often a family traveled this way: the father came first. He found a job and worked through the winter. When he had earned enough, he bought tickets for the rest of the family. These tickets were sent back to Europe as prepaid tickets. Then the rest of the

Canada did much advertising for immigrants after 1903. Here is a shop window full of advertising about Canada.

family could come over and join him in America.

Many people made use of the prepaid ticket system. This can be seen from a study of the passenger lists that were given to the authorities every time an emigrant ship left for America. Passenger lists from Gothenburg, for example, show that about half of the 60,000 people who left Sweden in the years between 1883 and 1886 were travelling on prepaid tickets. About a third of the Danish emigrants traveled on prepaid tickets.

The system of prepaid tickets shows how emigration can have a snowballing or self accelerating effect. Earlier emigrants pulled over an increasing number of later emigrants. The more people who emigrated to America from a given country, the more there were to pull others to America. Prepaid tickets, money orders sent back home, and encouraging letters from the New World were among the ways that immigrants used to attract their fellow countrymen to follow them.

The passenger lines supported this development. A little company like the Danish Thingvalla Line had 400 agents and subagents in the USA. They lived throughout the country, in cities and rural areas where Danes had settled. The big international lines like Cunard and White Star must have had tremendous numbers of agents and subagents all over America. The many foreign language newspapers, published throughout America before 1914, always contained advertisements for passenger agents. They offered help in sending tickets back to the homeland.

Advertisement for steamship and railroad tickets in a Danish American newspaper, 1885.

Why Did They Emigrate?

The Greatest Mass Migration in History

Why did John Smith and Mary Jones emigrate to America along with hundreds of thousands of their European brothers and sisters? The question of motivation has dominated the studies of scholars of migration throughout the whole world. Such a large migration had never taken place before in the whole of human history. Even more astounding is the fact that this migration crossed 4,000 miles of ocean.

This migration meant that the center of the world was shifted from Europe to America.

Push and Pull

Europe and America, the old and new worlds, developed a special relationship towards each other. On the one side was Europe, where social conditions resulting from industrial expansion and population explosion created an atmosphere of discontent among working peo-

Immigrants arriving in New York around 1900.

Mentally ill and retarded people were not allowed into the USA. Those who were suspected had to pass a test before they were allowed to enter the country.

ple in rural as well as urban areas. On the other side was America, with its immense tracts of uncultivated farm land and its tremendous untapped sources of energy and other resources, waiting for the manpower that was needed for further development.

Scholars have tried to measure both sides of the force that motivated emigration in order to determine which was the strongest. Was it the bad social situation in Europe that **pushed** people out, or was it the **pull** of forces from America, higher wages and greater opportunities?

When the number of emigrants, year by year, is compared with the curve of economic developments in Europe and America, it looks like the pull factor from America was stronger than the push factor from Europe. But figures alone cannot explain this mass migration. The historical context must also be studied. In actual fact, it was not a case of either push or pull, but rather of both working at the same time.

Information—and Ocean Liners

A huge ocean separates Europe from America: the North Atlantic. Emigration began at a time when Europe's population still lived in relative isolation. In some countries, most people could still not read and write. They had little opportunity to learn about life on the other side of the Atlantic. Given that situation, a mass migration to America could hardly have gotten started and reached such immense proportions without two key factors:

1. Somebody had to provide Europeans with information about the wonders of America, and
2. Somebody had to make it possible to cross the greatest obstacle to emigration, the North Atlantic Ocean, without such a high risk to life and limb.

In this perspective, we can see that transportation formed the key link in the movement of 52 million people from Europe to America.

The passenger lines were decisive in several ways. They were a channel of information. They had a system of agents and subagents that could spread information throughout Europe about the need for manpower of every kind in America. They created a fleet of steamships that could carry half a million people a year—in the years after 1900, more than a million a year—to America.

America letters, the letters from immigrants in the New World, were eagerly read in Europe. Often the schoolmaster or clergyman had to read them to illiterate villagers. Danish painting from 1835.

Where Did They Settle?

The passenger lines also influenced other factors for the stream of people emigrating across the Atlantic. They influenced where people came to settle in America.

Most of the big passenger lines had agreements with certain railroads. Emigrants who chose those passenger lines often ended up living and buying land from the same railroad. The fact that so many Scandinavians settled in Minnesota was due, among other things, to the Northern Pacific Railroad. It worked through the Cunard Line to attract Scandinavian settlers to Minnesota. The fact that there are still Danish settlements in New Brunswick is due to cooperation between the Allan Line and the local New Brunswick government authorities. Many other examples could be cited.

Pamphlet advertising 40,000,000 acres of land for sale along the Northern Pacific Railroad. This line was completed in 1881.

Ticket Prices Fall

Better opportunities for transportation was also a reason for a change in the kind of people who emigrated as time passed. The average age of emigrants kept getting lower. In the 1870's, many emigrants were between 30 and 40 years old. There were many families with children. After the

1890's, there were very few families. Most of the emigrants were young, unmarried men and women. This might be due to the fact that the price of the ticket to America kept becoming lower and lower while wages gradually became higher. Every time the ticket price fell, a younger and poorer segment of the population had the opportunity to emigrate.

In any case, 52 million Europeans would never have come to America if their transportation across the Atlantic had not been a good business for those who provided it. The emigration business gave good jobs to many people on both sides of the Atlantic.

Rural mailman in Crawfordville, Indiana, in 1899.

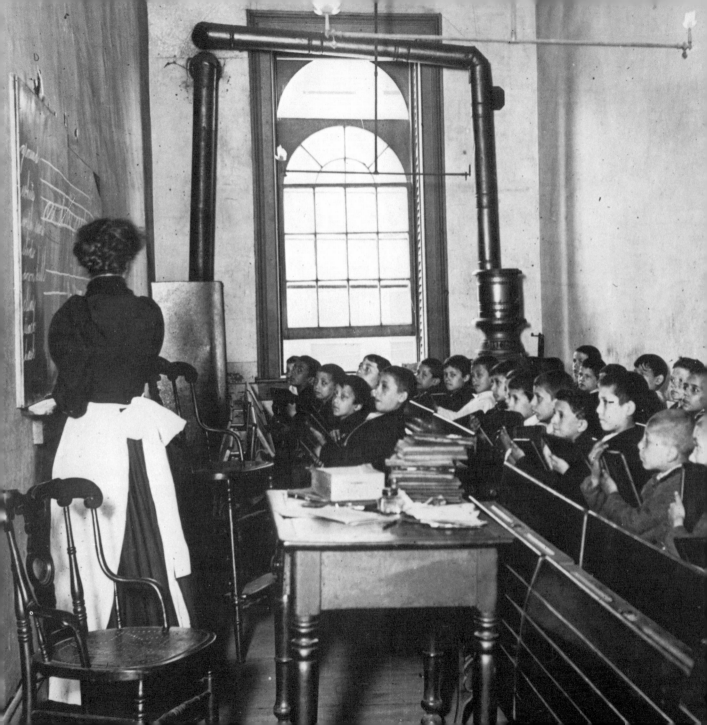

Learning to be Americans, 1888.

To help learn English, the immigrant could get a phrase book. They were printed in many languages, and some included phrases enough for several months of conversation. The only problem was that they did not give very good tips on pronunciation, and they did not teach how to think in English.

44

Jeg kan ikke læse uden Briller.	I cannot read without spectacles.
Anstræng ikke Deres Øine med at læse for fint Tryk.	Do not strain your eyes with reading small print.
Vogt Dem for at læse eller skrive i Aftenskumringen.	Beware of reading or writing in the dusk of the evening.
Jeg har været saa ufornuftig.	I have been so imprudent.
Vær forsigtig med Ilden.	Be careful with the fire!
Kan jeg fuldkommen stole paa Dem.	May I entirely rely upon you.
De kan være forvisset om, at jeg ikke skal være uagtsom.	You may rest assured, that I shall never be off my guard.
Drag Gardinerne sammen.	Draw the curtains to!
Nu er Alt færdigt, min Herre.	All is now ready, Sir.
Vil De have Deres Seng opvarmet?	Will you have your bed warmed.
Nei ikke i Aften.	No, not to night.

I et Hotel.   At a hotel.

Kan jeg forblive her i Nat?	Can I stay here to-night?
Vi have ikke noget Værelse ledigt.	We have no room disengaged.
Jeg ønsker et Værelse paa første Sal.	I want a room on the first floor.
Alle Værelser ere optagne undtagen et i Stueetagen.	All the rooms are occupied except one on the groundfloor.
Sig til Pigen, at hun giver mig Vand og Haandklæder.	Tell the maid-servant to bring me water and towels.
Ønsker De at spise til Middag paa Deres Værelse.	Should you like to dine in your room.
Hvad Tid spises til Middag her?	At what o'clock do they dine here?
Lidt efter Kl. 2.	A little past two o'clock.
Bær mine Sager til mit Værelse.	Bring my things to my room.
Tilhører denne Hund Dem?	Does this dog belong to you?
Nei den tilhører en Franskmand.	No, it belongs to a Frenchman.
Han var paa Dampskibet.	He was on board the steamer.

Index

Picture Credits